W9-BSH-795

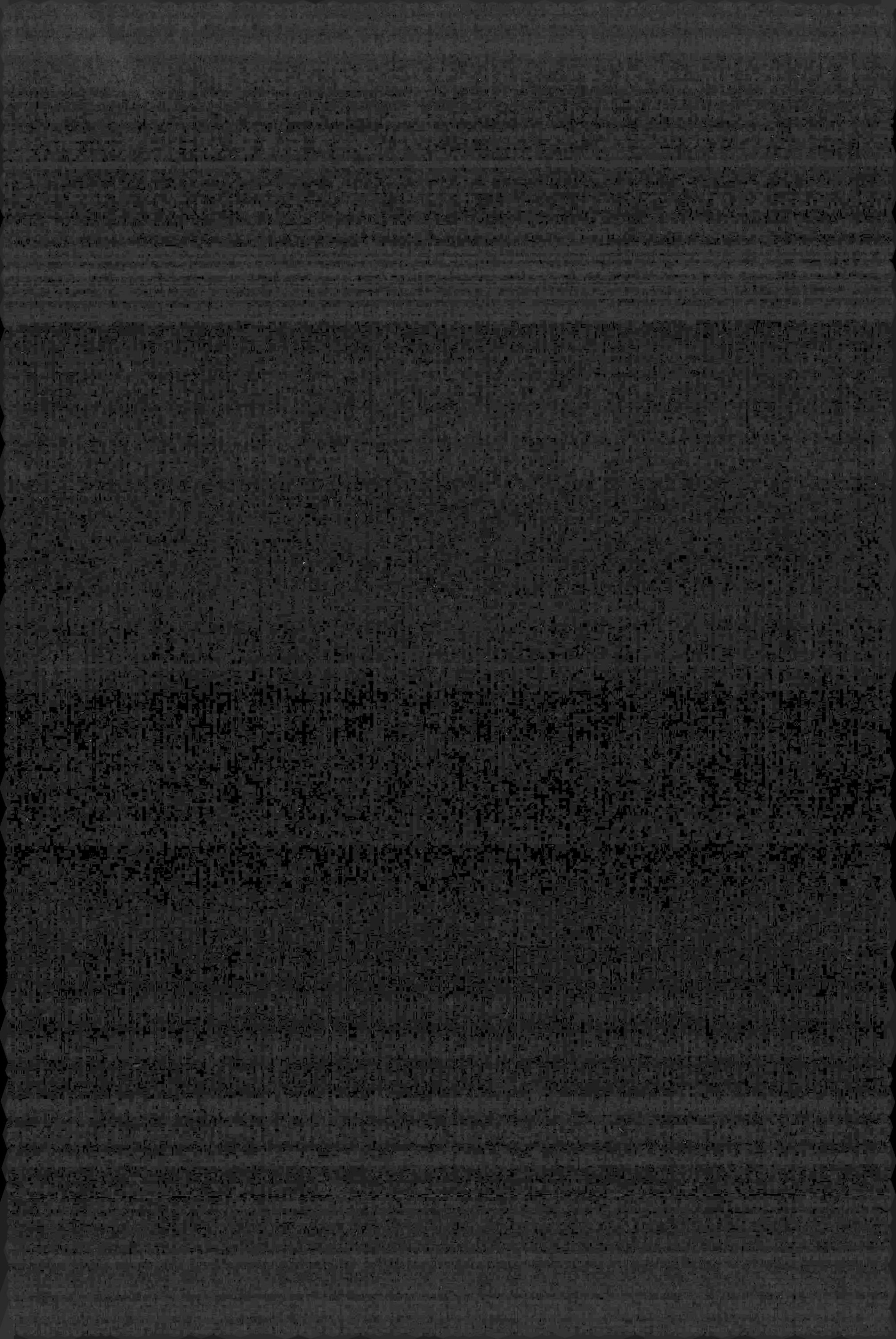

place hacking

VENTURING OFF LIMITS

michael j. rosen

TWENTY-FIRST CENTURY BOOKS / MINNEAPOLIS

Front cover: Bradley L. Garrett, a member of the urban exploration group known as the London Consolidation Crew, pauses on a crane above Aldgate East in London.

Back cover: When workers laid brick sewers in London in the 1880s, a unique oval- or egg-shaped tunnel housed the confluence of two larger sewers. Tunnelers and DrainOrs—two types of underground explorers—love to frequent these expanses.

Title page: A place hacker descends headfirst into the abandoned Embankment cable run, part of the tunnel system originally designed for transporting Londoners via underground cable cars.

Publisher's note: This book is intended to provide readers with information about the phenomenon of place hacking. It is not intended to be a how-to guide or to encourage participation in the activities described herein, and readers are specifically advised not to engage in those activities. The activities described in this book are inherently risky and may be in violation of applicable laws. Engaging in any of the activities described in this book may result in damage to property, serious injury, or death for the participant or others and may also result in substantial civil or criminal liability.

Except for the publisher's and author's websites associated with this book, the publisher and the author are not affiliated with and do not sponsor or endorse any websites, organizations, or other sources of information referred to herein and do not warrant the accuracy, completeness, or currency of any information or recommendations provided by those sources.

The publisher and the author shall not be liable for any damages allegedly arising from the information in this book, and they specifically disclaim any liability from the use or application of any of the contents of this book.

Acknowledgments: The author would like to thank Daniel Carlson, a Denison University summer intern, for his invaluable assistance in researching, documenting, and writing this book.

Twenty-First Century Books
A division of Lerner Publishing Group, Inc.
241 First Avenue North
Minneapolis, MN 55401 USA

For reading levels and more information, look up this title at www.lernerbooks.com.

Library of Congress Cataloging-in-Publication Data

Rosen, Michael J., 1954–
Place hacking : venturing off limits/ by Michael J. Rosen.
pages cm
Includes bibliographical references and index.
ISBN 978–1–4677–2515–6 (lib. bdg. : alk. paper)
ISBN 978–1–4677–6311–0 (eBook)
1. Explorers—Juvenile literature. 2. Adventure and adventurers—Juvenile literature. 3. Abandoned buildings—Juvenile literature. 4. Trespass—Juvenile literature. 5. Urban geography—Juvenile literature. I. Title.
G175.R66 2015
910.9173'2—dc23 2014003218

Manufactured in the United States of America
1 – BP – 12/31/14

CONTENTS

A NOTE FROM THE AUTHOR

I am an explorer, but not the sort featured in this book. I may be decidedly afraid of heights, but I am deathly afraid of edges. A friend used to joke that if someone dropped a square of black construction paper on the floor, I'd get dizzy. Moreover, I am what psychologists call conflict averse. I eschew confrontation. I'm a do-gooder, a law-abider.

So, up front, I admit it: I have utterly no street cred when it comes to this book. The deliberate choices to take frequent risks, to sneak into restricted zones, to climb up—or even down!—wobbly structures in the dark: these are not choices that I would make.

However, I *do* have writing creds. And I do consider writing a form of exploration.

Moreover, I'm a visual artist. So I can share the urban explorer's passion for seeing new perspectives and looking harder, looking beyond.

I'm also something of a discoverer (I'm a zoology major and a natural-history buff), so I bring an appreciation of the natural and built environments and of our abilities to adapt to and move through them.

And I'm a hiker. I figure I've walked the acres where I've lived for twenty years, with one or more dogs, close to fourteen thousand times. I devotedly believe that the familiar shouldn't be treated with less reverence than the unfamiliar. The concept of exploration cannot be the exclusive province of eighteenth-century explorers charting the New World or of modern oceanographers mapping the ocean floor or of astronauts conquering the frontiers of space. In fact, three-time NASA shuttle astronaut Dr. Kathryn D. Sullivan, one of the first six women to join the National Aeronautics and Space Administration astronaut corps and the first American woman

Rural, rather than urban, explorer Michael J. Rosen and his crew, an Australian Stumpy Tail Cattle Dog, live in the Ohio foothills of the Appalachians.

to perform a space walk, once told me: "That I have managed to conduct . . . explorations on the grand theaters of space, Antarctica, or the bottom of the Sea of Cortez is of the same nature as the discoveries we all make on smaller stages."

So exploration is not aimless wandering. It's the direction our minds take us, the means by which our experiences shape the instinctual creatures that we are. So now that space and the oceans have lost much of their emotional hold on us, where do humans find mysteries to pluck the imagination or new perspectives to beckon the inquisitive or impossible voyages to lure the fearless?

Around the globe, many people would say the answer is place hacking: urban exploration, adventuring in the built environment, or infiltrating a restricted structure or event. Passionate individuals would claim these are quests that can feed the human drive to be awed and challenged.

To these explorers, the very structures of civilization—whether under construction, in ruin, or even fully functioning and decidedly *not* welcoming unauthorized "explorers"—comprise the frontier that can inspire and embolden. To set foot inside one of these environments or buildings—or to tiptoe across a seven-story ledge or crawl through a ventilation system—melds the past with the present and questions the future of these particular sites.

The place hacker mission? To reexplore and to uncover a different aesthetic or alternative purpose in places that have already been designed and built, already hummed with human life and industry, and already outlived their original function.

Consider these pages to be less of a guidebook than a guest book. Less of a how-to handbook than a record of highlights in the history of this—well, what is it? A sport? An art? A political movement? A discipline with a deliberate lack of discipline? A crime?

You may decide that place hacking fits one, some, or all of those categories. As you'll discover, each participant chooses to explore both a built landscape as well as the moral landscape by which each personal choice is made.

—Michael J. Rosen

Much of the motivation to hack into a site is fueled by the chance to revel in spectacular views of cityscapes that even skydivers can't approach. Here, Bradley L. Garrett stands atop a derelict thirty-story skyscraper in London.

CHAPTER 1

What Is PLACE HACKING?

Having popped a few sewer lids to explore a bit of subterranean Paris, American adventurers Moses Gates and Steve Duncan decide to follow Nico, a guy they'd just met, to a cathedral he'd been eager to climb. They figured, why not, how hard could it be?

When the trio arrives at Notre Dame Cathedral, they use a makeshift scaffolding ladder to hoist themselves along the cathedral's outside walls and up one of the flying buttresses. Arriving at a locked terrace, they unscrew the lockset from the door and climb a spiral staircase to the bell tower. A carved menagerie of glaring imps and gargoyles monitors their every footstep. The view, from above the City of Lights, is stunning.

Gates describes the moment in his book *Hidden Cities*. "Tomorrow, there will be hundreds of tourists on the north tower looking right at where we are now. But none of them will know what it's like to look back."

□□□□□

From the central spire of Notre Dame Cathedral in Paris, urban explorer Steve Duncan took this elegant photograph of the city and the cathedral towers.

Documentation

Yet other place hackers seek to capture moments in time. Some photograph or videotape their explorations as proof that they were there. Others want to find and capture the beauty of decay or to reveal the unexpected magnificence of a grim industrial complex. Still others look for graffiti-layered prison walls. The goal for this type of documentary-style place hacker is sharing his or her views with comrades and with fans who stumble across their websites.

> **"When we see a sign that says DANGER: DO NOT ENTER we understand that this is simply a shorthand way of saying 'Leaving Protected Zone: Demonstrate Personal Accountability Beyond This Point.'"**
>
> *—Ninjalicious (Jeff Chapman), one of the earliest gurus of urban exploration and infiltration, 2005*

The Adrenaline Rush

Shimmy through broken windows. Crawl between gaps in locked fences. Turn invisible as a guard approaches. These exciting actions release the body's adrenaline, turning fear into energy. Some urban explorers say that their treks are also a form of personal liberation. These explorers long to walk the tightrope—at times, a literal tightrope—that stretches between safety and danger, between logic and craziness. It's a quest for the elation of being alive on the other side.

Just Because

Yet other place hackers say their reason for exploring a particular place is "because it's there." This was the motive of famous British mountaineer George Mallory, who climbed Mount Everest, the world's tallest mountain, in the 1920s. For this type of explorer, life is less about earning money and acquiring possessions than it is about chasing a dream. Author and place hacker Bradley L. Garrett says that if performing a "playfully unproductive, pointless . . . largely [unmarketable] action appeals to an individual—in the same way a swing or a pony ride appeals to a six year old—that explorer is free to make it happen." Picnic on top of a monastery, throw a graduation party in a deserted auto manufacturing plant, host an all-night meditation in an abandoned railroad tunnel—these are all "just because" actions.

At the completion of construction in 1929, Eastern State Penitentiary in Pennsylvania was considered the largest and most expensive public structure ever erected. Shut down in 1971 and abandoned until the late 1980s, the crumbling institution has since become a National Historic Landmark and is open for tours. This barber's chair is in a cell of the facility.

One Site Does Not Fit All

Just as the motivations for place hacking vary, so do the types of explorations. There are three main branches of place hacking. The first and most common is known as urban exploration, or urbex. It refers to the general investigation, documentation, or enjoyment of abandoned, ruined, or restricted spaces such as bridges, tunnels, and buildings.

The second, urban adventure, focuses on performing an action. This might include scaling a suspension bridge or leaping from it in a wingsuit (a jumpsuit that adds surface area to the body to increase lift), wading in waist-deep water in drainage tunnels, or staging an impromptu performance at a condemned site. These are more vigorous and rigorous adventures, often requiring training, equipment, and a bigger appetite for danger.

The third branch of place hacking is infiltration, or the exploration of a "live," still-in-use site. Typically, this involves research, disguise, technology, and other methods of gaining access to a restricted environment. Infiltrators might sneak into an engagement party or slip into the rooftop pool at a fancy high-rise.

Daredevil photographer and urban explorer Lucinda Grange stands sixty-one stories above midtown Manhattan on one of the Chrysler Building's eagle-head ornaments. Grange's specialty: defying security guards around the world to snap dramatic rooftop images.

CHAPTER 2 Urban EXPLORATION

After snapping a selfie from atop the Notre Dame Cathedral, Moses Gates suddenly realizes that he is poised for a once-in-a-lifetime opportunity. He manages to ring the cathedral's bells, just like Quasimodo, the hunchback hero of Victor Hugo's 1831 novel *The Hunchback of Notre Dame*.

Minutes later, the French police poke their heads into the bell tower and bellow a few words. Gates doesn't speak French, but he is certain the words mean something like "Hey, idiots! Don't move!" He shrugs at his fellow explorers and prepares to face the music.

Rooftopper Tom Ryaboi (pseudonym Roof Topper), took this aerial photograph of downtown Toronto, Ontario. The famous CN Tower is the red needlelike structure in the center. Ryaboi is a passionate photographer who says he intends to stand on every roof in the city to claim the view—even for just a few moments.

Toronto-based explorer Ninjalicious was one of the prime movers of urban exploration. He described urbex as a sort of "interior tourism that allows the curious-minded to discover a world of behind-the-scenes sights." Urban explorers search for structures or places within those structures that most people overlook or reject. They're looking for a chance to say that they've been to such a place and taken gobsmacking photographs.

So what exactly are the prized locations for urban explorers? TOADS: temporary, obsolete, abandoned, and derelict spaces. Temporary spaces—such as construction sites, tent cities for a concert, or fairs that live just a few short weeks—are in a transitional state. After dark or after hours, these areas cry out "playground!" to explorers who want to experience each and every stage of the site's existence, not just the finished, official version that eventually opens to the public.

By investigating these sites, explorers feel they give such spaces new life and new meaning, even if only temporarily.

Obsolete spaces are those that have outlived their intended use. They may be military bases or manufacturing plants that ceased operation or sprawling, empty mental asylums (psychiatric hospitals) from the early twentieth century. When these spaces lose their support or purpose, they shut down. Some are carefully vacated, while others are hastily evacuated. They are rarely kept up or guarded. By investigating these sites, explorers feel they give such spaces new life and new meaning, even if only temporarily.

The *A* of TOADS stands for abandoned spaces, or structures that are no longer in use but have not been torn down. These might include a mansion in a neglected neighborhood, a charter school that closed down, or an amusement park that's been eerily silent since the last kids were squealing on the roller coaster decades earlier. These spaces remain fixed in time while the neighborhoods around them evolve, either through renovation or wrecking balls. The appeal of an abandoned site? Urbex explorers cherish the sharp contrast between something that does not change and the ever-advancing pace of the world around it.

Top: *Some place hackers seek to point out troubling beauty in regions where disaster has struck. For example, this abandoned amusement park is in the city of Pripyat, Ukraine, which was officially abandoned in 1986 after a catastrophic explosion at the nearby Chernobyl nuclear power plant.*

Bottom: *Urban explorers typically do not vandalize or otherwise change the spaces into which they trespass. Graffiti is one of the significant and often striking forms of decay they witness. This industrial plant is among many abandoned factories in Detroit, Michigan.*

HAPPY BIRTHDAY
BRooks

This home, once a handsome structure in a viable community, now invites an urban explorer to consider how place and time continually evolve. Everything is temporary, despite the guise of permanence.

The *D* of TOADS stands for derelict spaces. While time may have preserved abandoned spaces, it has begun to destroy others. Examples might be an old manor with layers of mildewed wallpaper and ceilings open to the elements, a historic armory overtaken by kudzu vines, a hurricane-flooded bus depot, or a sandstorm-buried village. These sites are shadows of their former selves. They bluntly remind explorers that the destruction of these sites may be just around the corner.

And yeah, you got it. The *S* in TOADS just stands for spaces.

The Many Faces of Urban Explorers

Many explorers favor a niche within a specific type of TOADS and identify themselves with that niche. For example, focusing on the remains of industry from the 1900s, postindustrial explorers target the former glory of a specific era. They may investigate sprawling auto manufacturing ruins in Detroit, Michigan, or choose the abandoned hydroelectric power station under Niagara Falls. They may be drawn to the site where a parent or a grandparent once worked. Or they may want to revisit a site they toured on an elementary-school field trip: the Vlasic pickle plant! the Sara Lee bakery! These areas generally still contain large, impressive machinery or irresistible buttons, levers, and dials.

Some explorers prefer sites that are greater or grander than a single building. They favor ghost towns. For example, the German occupation of France during World War II (1939–1945) devastated many towns. One such place was the farming village of Aradour-sur-Glane, which remains in a state of ruin. The 1986 explosion of the Chernobyl nuclear power plant in Ukraine changed a wide swath of land and sea into a toxic wasteland. A massive earthquake in 2008 transformed Beichuan, China, into a desolate and still uninhabitable city. Such sites present a range of intriguing relics for some explorers.

Asylum seekers seek out abandoned large-scale psychiatric hospitals, once called mental asylums. It's popular in the United Kingdom, where state-run facilities for the mentally ill were closed down in the mid-twentieth century, when the government decided they were ineffective and too costly. With that decision, dozens of outdated facilities ceased operation. Residents were released to the care of their families or left to fend for themselves.

From 1897 until 2005, the mammoth William Birch Rankine power station near Niagara Falls converted the energy of flowing water into mechanical energy. Since then, it has been a favorite destination of urban explorers. These two images suggest something of the site's undiminished scale and grandeur.

Going Underground

While many explorers practice their art aboveground, others go underground. These folks are known as tunnelers. Abandoned mine shafts, utility tunnels for a hospital complex or university, and ancient catacombs (burial chambers) light up the internal radar of tunnelers.

The catacombs of Paris, which hold the remains of about six million people, have the distinction as the most visited underground zone among tourists and urban explorers alike. That's partly because Parisian authorities tend to turn a blind eye to explorers. And the Paris catacombs go on for 200 miles (322 kilometers), with every sort of twist, turn, and chamber. Place hackers point to the catacombs as the earliest site of urban exploration: In 1793 Philibert Aspairt attempted to navigate these dark recesses by candlelight in hopes of discovering a lost wine cellar. He never found the cellar and disappeared for eleven years, until his body was eventually found near one of the catacomb exits.

Place hackers often point to the catacombs of Paris as the earliest and still the ultimate site for exploration. The 200 miles (322 km) of tunnels are the resting place of some six million skeletons.

CHAPTER 3

Urban ADVENTURE

Hand over hand, explorer Alain Robert ascends, lifting his knees higher with each step up the sheer façade of Cheung Kong Center. Every so often, he pauses to scan Hong Kong below him. Ten stories up, he attaches an enormous yellow banner to the glass skyscraper. The banner reads "OneHundredMonths.org," the website for a climate-change campaign by the New Economics Foundation.

Robert briefly savors the moment and then continues his ascent upward, passing secretaries and maintenance staff and bank executives inside their offices. Some catch a glimpse of him and point. Some have no reaction at all. Most don't even see him. Robert considers these people "dead men," too busy or bored to realize what is happening around them.

On June 11, 2005, French urban climber Alain Robert ascended the sixty-two stories of the Cheung Kong Center in Hong Kong's Central District. As a free solo climber, his only gear was gripping aids: a bag of chalk powder for his hands and rubber shoes for his feet.

movements to cross from point A to point B, using only the available elements of the built or natural environment and the body's strength and mobility. A person who practices parkour is known by the French word *traceur* (for a male) or *traceuse* (for a female). They hurdle benches, bound from a table to a car roof to a garage roof, scale walls, slide down rails, or leap between buildings. Yes, exactly the slick moves you've seen action heroes perform in video games such as *Grand Theft Auto* and *Assassin's Creed*. Exactly the choreographed stunts featured in movies such as the 2006 James Bond remake, *Casino Royale*. Typical sites for parkour include parks, playgrounds, office buildings, discarded structures, or anything else that presents itself as a worthy challenge.

Buildering

Buildering is like rock climbing, except it involves scaling the outside of buildings and other constructions—without ropes, belts, crampons, or any other safety device. (Bouldering + building = buildering.) The first notable instance of free-climbing a man-made structure occurred in 1916. Harry Gardiner gained the nickname the Human Fly by scaling the fourteen-story Majestic Building, the second-tallest skyscraper in Detroit. He was famous for making these extraordinary ascents in ordinary clothes, without special equipment. In fact, he scrambled up more than seven hundred buildings in Europe and North America.

Depending on the type of structure a person selects, the buildering challenges can range from child's play to superhero feats. Climbers go solo or in a group, in broad daylight or under midnight's cloak. Buildering can be as simple as taking a running leap from one part of a stone jetty along the lake to another. Or it can be as complex as climbing to the bell tower atop a university library or to the top of a crane that's hoisting girders to a skyscraper.

And then there's the specialized realm of buildering known as rooftopping. This activity involves buildering to the uppermost heights of a structure and then snapping totally awesome photographs. Shooting down, down, down from the eaves of steel braces and struts too high for even pigeons to roost requires matching nerves of steel.

Top: ***For rooftoppers such as Tom Ryaboi, dangling their feet over a ledge that provides a breathtaking and unfamiliar perspective onto the streets of a familiar city such as Toronto creates the greatest rush of adrenaline.***

Bottom: ***This traceuse practices parkour on the campus of the University of Cambridge in England. She vaults, leaps, and swings over various structures to move quickly and efficiently through space.***

B.A.S.E. Jumping

What comes *after* climbing a structure? Either going back the way you came—total buzz kill!—or leaping! At least, that's the option for people who practice B.A.S.E. jumping. Carl Boenish founded this All-American extreme sport in 1978 at Yosemite National Park in California. The acronym stands for building, antenna, span, and earth—the four basic fixed objects from which practitioners jump, using a parachute or a wingsuit to slow the fall. It's risky for the same reasons that buildering is. All the same, thrill-seekers have created several particularly impressive stunts. Valery Rozov, for example, made a record-breaking jump in 2013 from the north face of Mount Everest. In a four-day climb, he reached an altitude of 23,687 feet (7,220 m) and leaped down to the Rongbuk Glacier at 19,521 feet (5,950 m). That's a jump of 4,166 feet (1,270 m)!

B.A.S.E. jumping has also enjoyed its fifteen minutes—er, seconds, really—of fame in action scenes in movies. The most famous might be *Transformers: Dark of the Moon* (2011) and James Bond films such as *A View to a Kill* (1985) in which the fabulous model/singer/actor Grace Jones flings herself from the Eiffel Tower. (Actually, it's stuntman B. J. Worth who "takes the fall.")

Extreme Ironing

And you thought ironing was only for military-academy cadets and stay-at-home parents. Think again! One of the most radical types of urban adventure—whether in the city, the suburbs, or more remote realms—is extreme ironing, or EI. This sport and performance art "combines the thrill of an extreme outdoor activity with the satisfaction of a well-pressed shirt." Participants—an elite corps known as extreme ironists (no irony there!)—search for new and thrilling places to test their talent at removing creases from laundered items. Locations might include the bumper of a moving taxi, a hang glider, water skis, or even under water. These modern-day Marco Polo launderers press the outer boundaries of wrinkle wrangling.

At the first Extreme Ironing World Championships in 2002, athlete-performance artists from ten nations demonstrated their ironing skills in a quintathlon. The five events include urban (iron in, on, or around a broken-down car), water (iron on a surfboard, a boat, or a floatation device while traveling the rapids of a river), forest (iron among the treetops), rocky (iron on a climbing wall [facing page]), and freestyle (iron in whatever manner will impress the judges).

The Washington Post *calls the congressional hearing—in which the two cite their Fifth Amendment right to* not *answer each and every question—a "blistering bipartisan tongue-lashing."*

Did the Salahis view their actions as urban infiltration or as a plain-old, unabashed, fame-seeking media stunt?

Like the Salahis, urban infiltrators use sly, manipulative skills to break into or crash live sites. That is, they slip into high-profile events or popular high-traffic sites such as national monuments and Olympic stadiums. They might target a glamorous Hollywood wedding or a concert at a magnificent historic train station turned party house. Infiltrators also love to crash historical landmarks such as the Statue of Liberty or the infamous Eastern State Penitentiary, a former prison in Philadelphia, Pennsylvania, where many of America's most notorious criminals were jailed.

Of course, any infiltrator who imagines that sneaking into the Statue of Liberty's torch might be as easy as sliding down a storm drain has another thing coming—most likely, handcuffs. Urban explorers and adventurers specifically choose *inactive* (derelict, unguarded) sites and prefer to follow the code of ethics, which forbids breaking and entering. However, the live sites that infiltrators choose are *actively* maintained and guarded. They're far less likely to have unlocked windows or broken doors. This means they allow for easy, though unauthorized, entrance—and, even more important, escape. And they are usually under some type of surveillance, whether by guards, off-site protection monitors, security cameras, or legitimate visitors.

NINJALICIOUS

The concept of infiltration was first addressed by Ninjalicious (Jeff Chapman), a founder of the early urban exploration movement. He explored the topic in depth starting in 1996 with his 25-issue self-published magazine, *Infiltration: The Zine about Going Places You're Not Supposed to Go*. He also authored what some consider to be the core-handbook of urbex, *Access All Areas: A User's Guide to the Art of Urban Exploration*. He also created a website that recruited new explorers and energized this loose community of adventure seekers. In fact, it was Ninjalicious who coined the term *urban exploration*. He helped establish the code of ethics, claiming that "genuine" explorers are "in it for the thrill of discovery and a few nice pictures." Ninjalicious died of cancer just months after his book was released.

The former inmate cells and other historic ruins of Eastern State Penitentiary in Philadelphia are popular among infiltrators.

Nothing Succeeds Like Faking It

Many infiltrations end in failure. It's tough *not* to get caught. But a few are exceptionally successful. In the months before the 2012 Summer Olympics in London, for example, two security breaches in the city were led by a group of urban explorers known as the London Consolidation Crew (LCC). In 2011 they infiltrated the under-construction Olympic Park in the dark of night. News and photos of the breach bounced among explorer blogs, creating something just shy of a national security uproar. And then, just months before the opening of the Summer Games, three members of LCC scaled the tallest building in the European Union, the Shard. It juts 1,017 feet (310 m) above London Bridge. At the time, it was considered the second most secure site in London—after the new Olympic Park. Yet three men were able to slip past a single guard and spend the night snapping photos high over London. Uploaded later, the images delivered another blow to the confidence of Olympic security forces.

Two strategies typically lead to infiltrator success. The first is to break the code of ethics and break in: cut bolts, pick locks, remove doors, or break glass. Most place hackers frown on this approach because it does not respect the code. And it makes what's supposed to be hard too easy. But many infiltrators can break into a place without actually causing damage. For instance, in April 2011, members of the LCC enjoyed a week of exploration in London's Mail Rail system, a sub-subway reserved for mail delivery. As Bradley Garrett, an LCC member, described it, "Night after night, we . . . stood on the edges of the tracks waiting for the current to shut off on the third rail before we turned the Tube [subway] tunnels into our playgrounds of delicious disorder."

The second strategy for success is to rely on the tricks of social engineering. A long-lived and well-documented tool of the scam or the hustle, *social engineering* is a broad term for cagey methods of changing observers' perceptions to gain access or information. Often this involves costumes, falsifying documents, and inventing likely and believable—but totally false—stories.

Blending into an environment is a natural survival instinct. And humans are wired to ignore what is familiar so they can pay more attention to whatever's strange and possibly threatening. When an object or a person appears to belong in an environment, we typically don't ask questions. The Salahis, for example, were attractive, wore the right clothes, and knew how

Shortly before the opening of the 2012 Summer Olympic Games in London, place hackers stole into Queen Elizabeth Olympic Park, considered until that time to be one of the most secure sites in the United Kingdom.

to talk to national leaders and their guests. No one suspected they were infiltrators.

Based on our expectations of normal, we make quick assessments of other people. If we see a man wearing a colorful Hawaiian shirt, sunglasses, and a camera, we think "tacky tourist," not "terrorist." When we see a person in a neon-orange jacket and a hard hat, we think "city maintenance worker"—someone who has every right to set up safety cones and enter a manhole. We don't automatically assume that person is an urban infiltrator popping the lid on another adventure.

Credibility props help infiltrators build a convincing cover. Towels, swimsuit, magazines, and suntan lotion: the likely stuff a legitimate hotel guest would bring up to the rooftop pool. Suit and tie, clipboard with official-looking papers, name tag: an outfit for crashing the MTV Music Awards. Successful infiltrators have the right props and can act, dress, and sound as if they belong.

Code Breakers?

Infiltration is problematic, even among place hackers. For instance, does breaking the code of ethics invalidate a successful infiltration? Is a place hacker still following the code if she gains access to a site through damage created by a previous visitor—say, a chain-link fence snipped with wire cutters or an alarm-system panel with its sensors ripped free? Does sticking to the code while accessing a site make an infiltration more legitimate?

It's complicated business. Ask any two explorers to define what they're up to, and you're likely to end up with two sets of objectives and ideals.

Members of the London Consolidation Crew spent many months exploring every corridor of the underground railway once used by London's Royal Mail. A small driverless train conveyed mail from 1927 until 2003, when service ceased.

CHAPTER 5

Staging an Urban EXPLORATION TREK

Usual kit for these [draining] expeditions is: waders, torch, helmet, hi-viz [high-visibility] jacket, drain keys [to pry open a manhole cover], camera, tripod. Take away the waders, you get wet. Take away the torch, you can't see. Take away the hi-viz and helmet and you're suspicious. Take away the drain key and you can't get in. Take away the camera and you can't take photos. Take away the tripod and you get wobbly ones.

—Winch, urban explorer and photographer, 2010

Normally the more impressive the location, the more difficult it is to get in. It usually involves lots of trips, trying out different methods and techniques until you get your Eureka moment.

—GES057, user name for a Guerilla Explorer member, 2011

Built in 1938, the Industrial Rayon Corporation plant in Painesville, Ohio, manufactured a synthetic fiber, viscose, that was heralded as synthetic silk and provided materials for various products during World War II. In 1980 the plant closed. Exposed to the elements, the structure (photographed here by Johnny Joo) welcomes every sort of visitor: rain, mold, rodents, feral cats, and urban explorers.

The German monastery of Saint Jozefsheim opened in 1913 to house six hundred mentally and physically disabled people. It served various functions over the decades. Since closing in 1992, urban explorers such as Bradley Garrett and his colleagues (pictured here with their gear) *have used it for overnight accommodations.*

Props and Provisions

Once explorers have chosen a site, formed a plan, and gathered a group, they assemble their equipment. Urban exploration can be as high tech or as low tech as the individual or group desires. Some adventurers love nothing more than lugging along cameras the size of a cannon or coolers crammed full for a midnight feast. Others scoff at those who carry more than the bare minimum. That bare minimum starts with a good flashlight and fresh batteries (to navigate the dark). Next on the list are a camera and a tripod (to document the event). And the final essential is a valid ID (in case the infiltrator is questioned by guards or other authorities).

Other common gear includes ropes, waterproof boots, a first-aid kit, maps, and a cell phone. Place hackers consider it a liability to carry lock picks, firearms, crowbars, Swiss Army knives, or anything else that police or other authorities would consider a weapon. Nix on spray paints or other tagging paraphernalia: vandalism = arrest.

Specific locations or activities may require specialized equipment. For instance, a second flashlight is essential in sewers, tunnels, and any other exploration in which dead batteries would spell d-i-s-a-s-t-e-r. Medical face masks to filter air are necessary for old manufacturing plants or other sites where place hackers might encounter asbestos. Thick work gloves and long pants and shirts are standard issue for negotiating razor wire or barbed wire. Climbers require ropes. Drainers need waders (waterproof pants). And B.A.S.E. jumpers need their heads examined, *plus* a wingsuit or a parachute.

Acceptance

Start to finish, place hacking presents difficulties—from physical challenges such as climbing ability, endurance, and agility to logistical and tactical challenges. Yet the most difficult step of all is accepting responsibility. Whatever it takes, all place hackers must acknowledge that they alone assume the risks that are part of any exploration. If they are injured, fined, or otherwise beset with misfortune, they must accept the consequences. If a rotted floorboard collapses, a scaffolding beam slips free, a guy wire breaks, a guard relocks a door, a strong wind causes a loss of footing or a handhold or the camera—there's no faulting the city or seeking damages from a building owner. Inhaling a hazardous chemical, wading through contaminated water, or encountering a poisonous creature: they're all potential dangers on the waiver any place hacker "signs" by boldly going off limits.

To set personal experience above the law is to accept that such actions may carry a hefty price. Each individual balances those risks with the perceived gifts and pleasures that such actions offer.

CHAPTER 6

An Interview with BRADLEY L. GARRETT

Dr. Bradley L. Garrett is an archaeologist, a well-known urban explorer, and the author of *Explore Everything: Place-Hacking the City.* This passionate book urges readers to reclaim closed, derelict, and abandoned urban sites and to consider them opportunities for exploration and play. He believes citizens need to take back the rights to their city. He champions the impulse to seize or borrow the built environment—in whatever state of construction, use, or ruin each structure may be—and to appreciate the potential of each.

In an interview with Garrett, I asked him to talk about his philosophy of urban exploration and what makes it such a passionate pursuit. What follows are excerpts from our conversation.

Bradley Garrett climbed to the top of the Shard in 2012, just prior to its completion in London. The 1,004-foot (306 m), eighty-seven-story building, designed by world-renowned Italian architect Renzo Piano, is the tallest skyscraper in the European Union.

MJR: Was this desire to investigate or break boundaries something that's been with you since you were younger? What fed this appetite for urbex?

BLG: I grew up in Southern California. When I was about twelve, I'd head into the city with my skateboard to find hidden spots—loading docks behind grocery stores or odd curbs and handrails—and turn them into recreational spaces. They assumed a more dangerous element than originally intended. I mean, sliding a board down a long handrail—something designed for safety—has to be one of the most unsafe things ever!

Once I got a car, I had to escape the sterile suburbs. I used to pile fuel canisters onto the car roof and drive into the Mojave Desert, looking for old mining camps and Native American petroglyphs. And I'd camp there, by myself, in the wilderness. I'm sure all this led toward my pursuit of a master's degree in archaeology. A desire to get in touch with history . . . beyond what's available right on the surface. And excavation of the ground . . . led to excavation of other kinds of spaces.

When I moved to London, I sought out folks who had an interest in this same type of stuff—naturally urban explorers. It seems to me that skateboarding, archaeology, and urban exploration all share this idea of finding something in the world that isn't immediately obvious.

MJR: Think of famous historic explorers such as Sir Francis Drake, James Cook, Neil Armstrong, or Jacques Cousteau. To be an explorer means to discover or uncover some place or space in the world for the benefit of others. Some would therefore conclude that urban exploration is just people double-daring one another to go somewhere and do something they're not allowed to do.

BLG: The urge to explore is a big part of what makes us human. All that's left to "see" of the ocean must be conducted by robots. Archaeological digs are expensive and set aside as an "expert" practice. Likewise, outer space is mostly inaccessible for all but a few. The only new things left to find are hidden around us in cities. Urban exploration presents a way for everyone who has the physical capabilities to explore. For free. Right in "your own backyard"—assuming you live in a city.

The first person to go to the South Pole, the North Pole, *and* Mount Everest is Erling Kagge. [In 1994 this Norwegian explorer became the first

Bradley Garrett poses atop the roof of the Palais de Justice in Brussels, Belgium. The government building is believed to be the largest secular construction of the nineteenth century.

person to complete all three expeditions, known by many as the Three Poles Challenge.] A few years ago, he said to me, "Look, if you want to accomplish something new, you have to do something like ski one-legged to the South Pole. I've been an explorer for thirty years. When I saw your photos of urban exploration, I thought, yes, this is what's left to find. Rediscover what humans have built and left behind."

And this requires that we push past the social constraints in the same way that explorers did when they first climbed Everest. When people first suggested climbing Everest [in the 1920s], others said, "That's crazy! You'll never do it! You'll die!" And yet climbers did it, despite the naysaying. I'd argue that in twenty years, urban exploration will be an everyday activity. There will be little stigma or shock associated with it.

Exploration for the sake of exploration is wonderful. It got us where we are as human beings.

MJR: You're standing on the edge of a fortresslike skyscraper in London that soars 364 feet (111 m) upward. You're watching the massive construction of the new Tube [subway] station. Your fellow explorer, Silent Motion, turns to you and says: "I keep coming back because I feel so alive up here. It's more real than real life." Why is it that—he? you? we?—can't feel alive "down here?"

BLG: The desire to explore for the sake of exploring, to take risks for the sake of the experience with little thought to the "outcome"—that's primal. It's natural. It's a childhood trait. Urban explorers are, in one sense, rediscovering those feelings of unbridled play, staying up all night, uselessly wandering, plotting, and doing—all of which leads to the creation of very thick bonds between fellow explorers. Play becomes a way of de-emphasizing the importance of work. Play frees us from the role of consumer. It liberates us from the dominating idea of making money.

MJR: How much of the appeal of urban exploration comes from its illegal nature? If a landmark were open to the public, would the place still appeal to explorers?

BLG: An interesting question. In Germany, they afford more weight to personal responsibility. For instance, at Landscape Park in Duisburg-Nord, an old industrial ruin, you donate a few euros, sign a waiver, and you can walk around, climb blast-furnace towers, rappel down old factory walls. Or not. You can also just take a guided tour. Or sit in the courtyard and drink coffee. If you get hurt there, that's your responsibility. It's a great model.

But most of us live in societies where lawsuits are rampant. Insurance and liability coverage mean that people aren't afforded—and subsequently don't accept?—much personal responsibility. And this causes a general anxiety from feeling that life is being guided all the time. This is why urban exploration can be so rewarding—almost relieving—because you're solely responsible for what happens to you after you make the decision to unplug yourself and jump the fence.

In 1991 Landschaftspark (Landscape Park) in Duisburg-Nord, Germany, became a public park on the grounds of a former coal and steel production plant. Since then visitors have been allowed to tour the site with guides or to sign a waiver, accept whatever personal risks they choose, and explore. For example, scuba divers move through old gas tanks filled with water, rock climbers scale the factory's concrete walls, and visitors gather in the piazza (square) or scale towers that were once part of the steel mill.

An urban explorer scales the Battersea Power Station in London, an abandoned coal-fired power station on the banks of the River Thames.

MJR: As a follow-up, is it danger and risk that make a site more worthy of exploring? Does easy access make a place less interesting to urban explorers?

BLG: American sociologist Stephen Lyng has studied skydivers. Jumping out of a plane, they typically think, "This is crazy! Jumping from a plane! It's crazy to expect some device—this parachute—is going to save my life." When SCUBA diving (something I've also done a lot of), a similar thought

crosses my mind: "I'm 20 meters [66 feet] under water, and the only thing keeping me alive is this tank on my back." Oxygen tank or parachute, you have to trust the person who prepared your equipment and go for it. Urban exploration takes it even further—no equipment required!

I think we live so much of our lives on rails, never off the beaten track. Decisions are made for us. In order to have some control over their lives, some people need to push back more than others, to take back control, to take the hazard that comes with being responsible for each move you make.

MJR: An explorer who calls himself youliveandyouburn says we suffer from prepackaged adventures. Any inherent dangers are now carefully minimized. Any independent spirit is conveniently bottled and passed out beforehand to the participants. Is it true that excitement these days is like an out-of-season vegetable in a convenient freezer pack that consumers simply need to thaw?

BLG: Even worse, we're constantly distracted by a virtual vegetable that we think is real but provides no nutrients. Video games let you explore alien planets, narrowly avoid death, and quest through the world searching for treasure and adventure. But as soon as the game is turned off, you're depressed. It creates an addiction that keeps you yearning for the virtual all the time to distract you from how boring everyday life is.

The difference with genuine exploration is that it stays with you. And you can share it. It's an authentic adventure. I think that's necessary. The virtual representations we're given—even totally immersive, 3-D games, whatever—they're just so much manufactured content that you just passively join in.

MJR: Some urban explorers believe that they—that we all!—have a right to firsthand experiences with the built environment. They argue, if it's a public space, paid for with public dollars, then anyone's entitled to it. Does that mean each of us can say what is and isn't our legal right?

BLG: I believe everyone has a right to engage with his or her environment. A right to play. To explore. Admittedly, even a skateboard, to be technical, damages the curb. But citizens who care about the environment—urban, suburban, rural, or wild—have to be embedded in the places we live. If

> **"Architecture should be mortal. And if rubble, or even stories, are all that's left, that's a beautiful conclusion."**
> —*Bradley L. Garrett*

every environment is sterile, the world becomes horribly boring. That's not good for us. And that's not good for places.

And let's be clear: Places are always being lost. Because of war. Or catastrophic weather. Or because we love them to death. But culture is a renewable resource. We can rebuild. New stories can be told. And we can keep our eyes open to see where those stories are being told.

Preserving great monuments of civilization shouldn't be like buying a couch and keeping it covered in plastic so that no one can enjoy it or appreciate it. By the time the plastic comes off, the couch looks dated: a sad, well-maintained, unloved thing that must be replaced. We do this same thing to artifacts in museums—what's the point? (I know, not everyone agrees with me.) I say, if hundreds of millions of people come to see a particular site and it erodes or destabilizes and collapses, then that's a great ending to a magnificent history. Architecture should be mortal. And if rubble, or even stories, are all that's left, that's a beautiful conclusion to the story.

MJR: So, at some level, urbex becomes a challenge in personal ethics, personal politics, doesn't it?

BLG: It's making difficult decisions about rules: Are they there for sound reasons or for reasons that don't—or no longer—make sense? Coming to a conclusion like that requires critical thinking. Being an urban explorer requires that you not take things at face value. You must look at where your morals lead you so that you can go deeper. Everything we do in life should be a negotiation in that spectrum. Otherwise? We're all just pieces in someone else's game, with no will of our own.

MJR: Last question: As an urban explorer, you're something of a rebel journalist, underhandedly recording what you've seen. You have a blog, where you post your images with narratives. You've written articles and a comprehensive book. Is it fair to say you're a man on a mission?

Bradley Garrett stands on the rooftop of the Ritz-Carlton Chicago, a hotel in downtown Chicago, Illinois. His philosophy of place hacking is to discover what is hidden from plain sight.

BLG: My blog posts are meant to inspire. People comment, "I wouldn't ever do this, but it's great that you're doing this." Those replies are all the more powerful when you do something that's supposed to be impossible. When we climbed the Shard—London's tallest building—people said, "That isn't allowed; it's supposed to be impossible." And yet we did it anyway and we shared the view with others and that rewires what is thought to be possible.

When I started exploring, the way I thought about space and how it was structured and what I could do in it quickly changed. Everything became an opportunity: manholes suggested adventures; fences and locks meant interesting stuff inside to see; scaffolding offered a means to climb. And I have to admit: It's hard to reign in that impulse. Once you dig your hands into genuine discovery, you can't ignore it anymore.

PLACE HACKING TIMELINE

1793: By candlelight, Frenchman Philibert Aspairt explores the Paris underground—catacombs created by the haphazard quarrying of stone used in the city's great buildings such as Notre Dame Cathedral and the Louvre Museum. Legend says his quest was to uncover an ancient wine cellar. Eleven years later, he is found dead near one of the catacomb's exits.

1861: French photographer Nadar (Gaspard-Félix Tournachon) takes pictures of the new Paris sewer system, unintentionally becoming one of history's first drainers. He not only pioneered the use of artificial lighting in photography, but he was also the first aerial photographer, shooting from hot-air balloons.

American poet Walt Whitman visits the just-closed Atlantic Avenue Tunnel in Brooklyn, New York. Of this locomotive railroad tunnel, built in 1844, he later writes that it is "now all closed and filled up, and soon to be utterly forgotten, with all its reminiscences."

1900: British climber and poet Geoffrey Winthrop Young publishes the book *The Roof-Climber's Guide to Trinity*. In it, he describes for readers how to climb the buildings at Trinity College in Cambridge, England. This is considered one of the earliest examples of a word that nearly everyone has to look up: *stegophily*, or the art of climbing the outside of buildings. Most people use the word *buildering* instead.

1904: The New York Subway System opens to passengers on October 27. One week later, Leidschmudel Dreispul, a resident of the Bronx, explores the new tunnels and is killed by a passing train. As a result of his death, the city places No Trespassing signs throughout the system.

1916: The first celebrated builderer, Harry H. Gardiner, climbs fourteen floors and 223 feet (68 m) up the side of the Majestic Building in Detroit, Michigan. Traffic stops in all directions, and Gardiner earns the nickname the Human Fly.

1923: Following three buildering deaths, many cities in the United States ban the activity. That same year, the comedy film *Safety Last!* is released. It stars the silent-film legend Harold Lloyd, who dangles above the traffic from the hands of a clock mounted on the side of a skyscraper.

1937: Noel H. Symington, under the pseudonym Whipplesnaith, publishes *The Night Climbers of Cambridge*, an account of his daredevil scrambles atop the roofs of Cambridge University buildings. Lugging heavy camera equipment up drainpipes and across rooftops, his secretive and reckless club charted the entire skyline of the college and the surrounding buildings.

1950s: The Letterist International (LI), a group of young avant-garde artists and intellectuals, introduces the practice of the *dérive* (French for "drift"). In these outings, individuals took unplanned tours through the urban environment, directed only by whatever emotions or encounters the surroundings evoked.

1959: Members of the Tech Model Railroad Club at the Massachusetts Institute of Technology (MIT) in Cambridge take study "breaks" into campus steam tunnels and onto nearby rooftops. They dub this practice *hacking*. (Six years later, other MIT folks apply the term to cracking computer codes.)

1971: Twenty-year-old tightrope walker Philippe Petit of France crosses a high-wire he secretly stretched between the two spires of Notre Dame Cathedral in Paris.

1974: Petit duplicates his high-wire stunt, this time walking eight times across a 135-foot (41 m) cable attached between the two towers of New York City's World Trade Center. He later writes an account of this escapade, *To Reach the Clouds: My High Wire Walk between the Twin Towers*. In 2008 British filmmaker James Marsh's documentary *Man on a Wire*, based on Petit's book, wins an Academy Award for Best Documentary.

1977: New York toy maker and mountain climber George Willig scales the south tower of the World Trade Center in about 3.5 hours using a self-made climbing device. He is fined $250,000. New York mayor Abraham Beame reduces the charges to $1.10, or $0.01 per floor.

1978: Parachuting from tall rock formations known as El Capitan in California's Yosemite National Park, Carl Boenish, a local cinematographer, lays the groundwork for what will become B.A.S.E. jumping.

1986: In Melbourne, Australia, teen urban explorers known by aliases Dougo, Sloth, and Woody form the influential drainer group Cave Clan to explore caves and built structures.

1990: Vadim Mikhailov founds the Russian exploring group Diggers of the Underground Planet. Members roam subterranean Moscow, exploring bunkers, graves, caverns, and underground waterfalls, as well as abandoned subway, drainage, and sewer tunnels.

American outdoor enthusiast Alan S. North publishes a humorous manual on buildering, balancing, adventure biking, spelunking (exploring caves), climbing, and parachuting in the built environment. Titled *The Urban Adventure Handbook*, it popularizes the term *urban adventure*.

1996: Toronto-based urban explorer Ninjalicious (Jeff Chapman) publishes the first of twenty-five issues of *Infiltration: The Zine about Going Places You're Not Supposed to Go*. Coining the term *urban exploration*, he covers topics ranging from stealth and concealment techniques to ethical issues and legal consequences.

University of Minnesota student Max Action forms the group Adventure Squad for two reasons: as an alternative to the dull campus social scene and as a chance to locate the steam tunnels rumored to run under university grounds. Eventually, the members map the interconnected utility tunnels between Minneapolis and Saint Paul.

1997: Berliner Unterwelten (Berlin Underworlds Association) is founded by professors, craftspeople, police officers, lawyers, and a host of others interested in the uncharted territory of the air-raid shelters; deserted tunnels; caverns; brewery vaults; and bunkers in Berlin, Germany.

2001: The French film *Yamakasi: Les samouraïs des temps modernes (Samurais of Modern Times)* introduces the roof-leaping, wall-vaulting, trespassing, high-energy art of parkour to a broad global audience.

2002: The first recorded large-scale, Internet-facilitated meeting of worldwide urban explorers takes place in Brooklyn in the spring. The day is organized by the LTV Squad, New York City's oldest exploration team.

The first Extreme Ironing World Championship is held in Germany in September. Ten nations compete in five events: urban (ironing + broken-down car), water (ironing + fast-flowing river), forest (ironing + treetop), rocky (ironing + climbing wall), and freestyle (ironing + imagination). Great Britain takes first place.

2004: A second international urban explorer meetup takes place in Toronto, Ontario, in June. Humorously called Office Products Expo 1994, it provides four days of seminars, social events, expeditions, and general mischief (beginning with the name of the conference).

In October, Alain Robert, known as the French Spider-Man, scales the 614-foot-tall (187 m) headquarters of Total, the French oil company, near the center of Paris, wearing a Spider-Man costume.

2005: Canadian explorer Ninjalicious publishes *Access All Areas: A User's Guide to the Art of Urban Exploration*, a book that becomes the go-to guide about urban exploration and infiltration.

UX (Urban eXperiment), a French group of explorers focused on improving hidden Paris, sneaks into the Panthéon. This eighteenth-century church functions as a mausoleum for the remains of notable French citizens such as scientist Marie Curie and novelist Victor Hugo. The explorers' goal? To restore the 1850 clock in the building's bell tower. They are arrested and eventually tried for trespassing. Charges are dismissed.

2011: The London Consolidation Crew explores every abandoned Tube station in London and later the Mail Rail system, the underground railroad used by the postal system from 1927–2003.

2013: Russian daredevil Valery Rozov breaks the world record for the highest B.A.S.E. jump. He leaps from the north face of Mount Everest, landing almost a full minute later on the Rongbuk Glacier below.

2014: The exploring team of Russian Vadim Makhorov and Ukrainian Vitaliy Raskalov (both pseudonyms) of ontheroofs posts a short video on YouTube. It shows the duo climbing one of the world's tallest buildings, China's Shanghai Tower, without ropes or harnesses. They ascend 2,132 feet (650 m) by shimmying suspended poles and grabbing grates on the unfinished structure.

GLOSSARY

B.A.S.E. jumping: the idea of leaping from something other than a plane or helicopter was popularized in the 1970s. Modern B.A.S.E. jumpers now either wear wingsuits or parachutes to slow their descents from nonflying structures such as skyscrapers, bridges, or mountains. B.A.S.E. stands for building, antenna, span, earth.

buildering: to climb a building's exterior, with or without ropes or other tools. The term is a word blended from *bouldering*, another word for rock climbing, and *building*.

Cave Clan: an Australian group of drainers, founded in 1985, and one of the largest urban exploration groups in the world

credibility prop: an item that an infiltrator will carry or wear to mimic someone who belongs in a given place

crew: a group of urban explorers who work together

extreme ironing: a sport in which participants must iron a garment on an ironing board in an interesting, implausible, or dangerous place

key: an object, such as a crowbar or a door or a sewer key that urban adventurers use to gain access to a restricted, locked area

parkour: a discipline that emphasizes precise and practical movements made in awareness of one's surroundings in order to move from point A to point B with utmost speed. Parkour was founded in the late 1980s in France.

place hacking: to infiltrate or manipulate a public or privately owned space for personal purposes; a related group of extreme hobbies that emphasize investigating the built environment—particularly those structures that are closed, inaccessible, or abandoned

social engineering: a system of methods used to gain unquestioned access to a site, an event, or information by changing observers' perceptions of what is expected or normal

TOADS: this acronym refers to the four kinds of sites that urban explorers target for their adventures. They are temporary, obsolete, abandoned, and derelict spaces.

traccur: a male practitioner of parkour. A female practioner of parkour is called a traceuse. The terms are French and refer to tracing, or making, a path.

urban adventure: this branch of place hacking steps beyond exploration, using the environment for additional physical or creative challenges

urban exploration: this branch of place hacking involves recreational trespass into abandoned or ruined buildings; also called urbex or UE

urban infiltration: this branch of place hacking is performed at an active site and typically requires encountering or interacting with others at a site or event to which a person has not been invited

waders: waterproof pants usually worn by fishers, often used by people exploring drains, caves, or sewers

wingsuit: a specialized bodysuit with fabric that stretches open between the arms and the torso. The suit allows skydivers and B.A.S.E. jumpers to descend more slowly.

PERSUASIVE WRITING ACTIVITY

Electrifying stories! Exhilarating expeditions! Extraordinary vistas! Focus as they may on the positive, in some instances, place hackers must admit their actions are illegal. Why do they do what they are doing? Is there a point when a recreational romp becomes an unreasonable risk? Is personal safety entirely one's own judgment?

Working alone or with classmates and friends, look more closely at the interview with Bradley Garrett, one of the best-known urban explorers. Are his ethical arguments about urban exploration and trespassing convincing? Why or why not? Write a persuasive essay supporting your views. Try to include supporting material from other reputable sources.

To further investigate these complex issues, consider the following incidents of place hacking. Beneath each scenario are further justifications. Which perspective seems most persuasive? Write a narrative essay arguing your point of view.

DILEMMA #1: DOES A POSITIVE OUTCOME JUSTIFY HACKING?

An exploring duo decides to stay overnight in a closed-down, off-limits tower that was once part of a college dorm. Their claim: "We admit we hacked into the site. We even admit to using bolt-cutters on the padlocks. But we feel that, through breaking into the tower, we revealed a security breach that the university should address. If anything, they should be grateful for what we did."

Consider these counterarguments:

- Who asked the pair to look for security breaches? The argument is a little like a firefighter setting a building ablaze just to prove that the building was vulnerable to arson. Adventurers can't just do whatever they want and then expect people to thank them, especially if what they do is illegal.
- Even though the pair broke into a site illegally, their actions were not harmful in any way. Had someone else with intent to do damage broken into the tower, that person might have created damages worth millions of dollars. Hacking without damaging a site is okay.
- If the explorers really wanted to help out the university, they could have sent an e-mail or a letter. Just because the adventure revealed a bigger problem does not suggest that the behavior is worthy of praise.

What argument finally persuades you and why?

DILEMMA #2: NO HARM, NO FOUL?

An explorer has just returned from photographing a grand, long-abandoned theater. She claims: "So what if I trespass? As long as I don't break anything to get in or damage the place while I'm there, what's the big deal? Come and go—no one knows."

Consider these counterarguments:

- Whether or not she breaks anything, she has no right to go where she's not permitted. Justifying one crime by saying she didn't commit a worse one is stupid.
- How can it be a crime if no one gets hurt and the place looks exactly the same as before she explored it? The site isn't being used. It's already damaged and probably slated to be torn down.
- She may not have broken the lock or the door through which she entered, but she took advantage of an activity that she knows breaks the law for nothing more than her own personal amusement.

What argument finally persuades you and why?

DILEMMA #3: IS A LIE COMMITTED IF IT'S NOT TOLD?

An infiltrator steals into the annual Governor's Ball after the Academy Awards. He claims: "My business cards don't say that I'm a press photographer. I had a camera. I gave the security guards my card. Is it *my* fault they gave me a press pass and let me in? Am I under an obligation to correct people? I don't think so."

Consider these counterarguments:

- He might not have told a lie at any point, but that is only because he manipulated the situation so that he wouldn't have to. There are two kinds of lies: commission and omission. So he didn't *tell* a lie; he *didn't tell*—and that's a lie.
- Lying is not illegal unless offered to a legal authority such as a judge or a police officer. Since he did not actually *lie* on his business card or scrawl a fake name on a sign-in sheet, he's fine, legally speaking.
- I can think of a dozen things that I can get away with *legally* but that are ethically contemptible. If his presence caused trouble, those guards could very well be fired for letting him in.

What argument finally persuades you and why?

FOR FURTHER INFORMATION

BOOKS

Garrett, Bradley. ***Explore Everything: Place-Hacking the City.*** New York: Verso Books, 2013. This 380-page, illustrated book brings together Bradley Garrett's PhD dissertation about place hacking; his blog/website; and his escapades with the London Consolidation Crew, an urban-exploration collective. Garrett's work is a thoughtful exploration of philosophy, politics, and adventure.

Paiva, Troy. ***Night Vision: The Art of Urban Exploration.*** San Francisco: Chronicle Books, 2008. Often inspired by derelict sites, Troy Paiva (who goes by the name Lost America) is a professional photographer who specializes in night painting. This camera technique allows the artist to create atmospheric images by using various sources of illumination to "paint" light into an image while a camera's shutter is open. This book presents Paiva's photographs and commentary on a range of sites.

Whipplesnaith. ***The Night Climbers of Cambridge (The Cult Classic Bible of Buildering, Bouldering, Climbing, Free Running and Parkour)***. Cambridge, UK: Oleander Press, 2010. Available as an e-book through Amazon Digital Service, this account by Whipplesnaith (the pseudonym of Noel H. Symington) was published in October 1937, chronicling his year of nighttime exploits with fellow students on the roofs of Cambridge University. Their feats included scaling heights such as the Fitzwilliam Museum and King's College Chapel, while lugging heavy, primitive camera equipment. The e-book includes seventy digitally remastered images.

WEBSITES

The following websites are as accurate and up to date as possible. Many place hackers, wishing to protect their anonymity, use pseudonyms or post anonymously and often manipulate the content of their sites, which are not necessarily permanent.

Abandoned UE
http://www.uerev.com/index.php?pid=home
This photo-based website shares reviews of various urban exploration outings in New York; Michigan; and Ontario, Canada. Members of the website document their experiences, writing about successes, failures, and high points of each trek.

Abandoned USA
http://www.abandonedusa.com
This site features photographs and documents of abandoned places in the United States, including the ghost town of Salton City, California; the Six Flags amusement park in New Orleans, Louisiana, destroyed in Hurricane Katrina in 2005; and a "haunted" state hospital for the insane in Indianapolis, Indiana. It is the project of photographer Kris Arnold, who writes, "Many of the locations are demolished or will soon be demolished and this project is a means to preserve the history of these places in their final days and be a constant reminder that nothing we build or construct lasts forever."

Adventure Worldwide
http://www.adventureworldwide.net
This website offers a range of place-hacking stories and photographs from around the world. Explorations in each country present unique opportunities and demands.

Guerilla Exploring
http://www.guerrillaexploring.com
This site hosts an impressive array of stunning photographs and place-hacking stories. It includes a range of explorations, including draining, infiltration, and rooftopping. Contributors are anonymous.

Undercity
http://www.undercity.org
This is the website of urban historian Steve Duncan, whose primary interest is unpeeling the layers of a city. His particular interests are sewers and drains. The site features short documentaries by Andrew Wonder of Duncan's explorations in New York City and Las Vegas, as well as his lecture at TEDx Phoenixville 2012, and slide shows of his urbex photography.

Urban Ghosts: Hidden History and Offbeat Travel
http://www.urbanghostsmedia.com/category/urban-exploration/abandoned-buildings-places/
This online source features news about abandoned places, hidden history, and offbeat travel. The "abandoned" subject areas, all of which include breathtaking photos, are buildings, places, vehicles, vessels, and urbex/infiltration stories.

The Winch
http://www.thewinch.net
This website was created by the Winchester, a London-based urban photographer and explorer who worked with Bradley Garrett in his research. Winch's site contains examples of particularly good photographs of his current and past excursions, as well as links to other explorers' sites and books he's found influential.

VIDEOS AND FILMS

***Man on a Wire*, 2008.**
This film by James Marsh chronicles Philippe Petit's 1974 high-wire walk between New York's Twin Towers at the World Trade Center. It is based on Petit's book *To Reach the Clouds*.

Place Hacking: Exploring Everything
http://www.vimeo.com/channels/placehacking
This series of videos was created by Bradley Garrett and is also featured on his website.

UE Kingz's Videos
http://www.vimeo.com/user4368153/videos
Go to this site for music videos of urbex by the UE Kingz, a musical group that raps about exploration. Their song, *You Have to Choose*, serves as their explanation as to why they explore.

***Undercity*, 2011**
http://www.youtube.com/watch?v=vWF3IDk9Gek
A twenty-eight-minute documentary, directed by Andrew Wonder, featuring urban explorer Steven Duncan in the subway system of New York City.

Urban Exploration
http://www.youtube.com/channel/HCUYSzuZAnyWU
YouTube contains more than seventy-five hundred videos on an Urban Exploration channel that it continually generates from user uploads. These range from highly produced and professional documentaries to hastily made and poorly lit snippets.

INDEX

PHOTO ACKNOWLEDGMENTS

The images in this book are used with the permission of: © Bradley L. Garrett, pp. 1, 6–7, 48, 50, 53, 55, 59; © John Kershner/Alamy, p. 3; courtesy of the author, p. 4; © Steve Duncan, pp. 8–9; © Nicholas Pappagallo Jr/Pixels.com, p. 15; Alex Shaw/Barcroft Media/Landov, pp. 16–17; Tom Ryaboi/CBE/ZOB/WENN.com/Newscom, pp. 18–19; © Pascal Le Segretain/CORBIS, p. 21 (top); © Cynthia Lindow/Alamy, p. 21 (bottom); © Shaun Lowe/Vetta/Getty Images, p. 22; © Jonathan Castellino, pp. 23 (left), 23 (right); © Rieger Bertrand/hemis.fr/Alamy, pp. 24–25; © Sovfoto/UIG via Getty Images, p. 26; Mike Clarke/AFP/Getty Images/Newscom, p. 28; © Jayme Thornton/Digital Vision/Getty Images, p. 31; Tom Ryaboi/CBE/ZOB/WENN.com/Newscom, p. 33 (top); © Extreme Sports Photo/Alamy, p. 33 (bottom); AP Photo/Frank Mîchler, p. 34; © Samantha Appleton/White House via Getty Images, p. 36; © WIN Initiative/Getty Images, p. 39; © Lucy Sparrow, pp. 41, 56, © Dan Salisbury, pp. 42–43; © Photograph by Johnny Joo, p. 44.

Front cover: © Bradley L. Garrett.

Front jacket flap: © Oktay Ortakcioglu/Photographer's Choice RF/Getty Images.

Back cover and back jacket flap: © Mark Lovatt/Moment Open/Getty Images.

Main body text set in Conduit 11.5/15. Typeface provided by ITC.

ABOUT THE AUTHOR

Michael J. Rosen is the author of more than one hundred books for readers of all ages, including nonfiction, humor, poetry, young adult novels, anthologies, and picture books. His most recent nonfiction title for young adult readers is *Girls vs. Guys: Surprising Differences between the Sexes*. He lives in the foothills of the Appalachians in central Ohio. His website is www.fidosopher.com.